Handmade
Renaissance Faire
Fashion

20+

Patterns for Crafting Faire-Ready Capes, Cloaks and Crowns—
the Authentic Way!

Mara A. Vicario *and*
Maria Angeles Guisado (Alassie)

Creators of Costurero Real

PAGE STREET
PUBLISHING CO.

PAGE STREET
PUBLISHING CO.

First published in 2023 by
Page Street Publishing Co.
27 Congress Street, Suite 1511
Salem, MA 01970
www.pagestreetpublishing.com

Distributed by Macmillan, sales in Canada by The Canadian Manda Group.

27   26   25   24   23   1   2   3   4   5

ISBN-13: 978-1-64567-879-3
ISBN-10: 1-64567-879-2

Library of Congress Control Number: 2022952194

Cover and book design by Laura Benton for Page Street Publishing Co.
Photography by Alassie

Printed and bound in China

For those who believe in fairy tales.

Table of Contents

Introduction

Costurero Real is a Spanish alternative fashion brand with more than 12 years of adventure creating fantasy costumes for free spirits. We are proud that many of our customers have taken our designs to practically every Renaissance faire in the world, as well as to other incredible festivals, parties and events. Our fantasy costumes have even appeared in plays at theaters, video clips and so many other artistic manifestations of this rich creative scene.

While we love historical costumes and know and admire them, our inspiration has always been nature in the broadest sense (its colors, textures, smells and the richness of living beings) as well as fairy tales—traditional, folkloric or fantastic—transmitted through the culture of each country, by word of mouth or through the hand of fantasy authors throughout history. So, through this book of tutorials, we hope to be able to transmit our love for these themes, hand in hand with some characters that we find very representative.

It should be noted that the result of the creative processes contained in this volume might not look the same as the products we usually sell, because in our workshop, we work with professional tools such as laser engraving cutting machines, industrial riveting machines, molds and fabric sublimation machines. We have adapted the tutorials so you will be able to follow them easily at home, with tools that you could find anywhere and tips and tricks adapted for home use.

Enjoy with us the magic of creating!

The Fantasy and Fairy-Tale Look for a Ren Faire

There are many Renaissance faires that require attendees to wear a historical costume of a certain rigor, but there are even more where you can attend wearing a fantasy outfit and where the creativity of each attendee is the only thing that sets the limit.

Many of our designs have a clear historical inspiration, but many others are directly inspired by traditional fairy tales or fantasy creations. The inspirations outside of historical rigor provide a lot of freedom concerning materials, fabrics and techniques.

In each chapter, and especially at the end of the book, you will see that with the same patterns but different colors and/or materials (fabrics, paints, decorations), you can adapt the pieces to achieve a more historical or more fantastical result; the same design can serve as the costume of a human, an elf, a fairy and so on.

We recommend you read through the whole book before starting to design your outfit, because you will discover that you can combine different elements of each chapter or character to create a completely new one.

Remember that, in a Renaissance faire look, the accessories are very important and often make the difference, so you will find in this book many techniques to make leather or resin pieces and putties that can be easily customized to take your outfit to the next level.

We hope you let your creativity fly and enjoy the process of creating your character for a Renaissance faire or any other event that you want to attend wearing our designs.

Tools For Crafting

For Fabric

1. Good fabric scissors (not just a regular pair of scissors)
2. Chalk to mark the fabric
3. Measuring tape, pins and needles
4. A sewing machine that can do stitching and zigzag; if you can get an overlock, all the better

For Leather

1. A leather cutter or a good scalpel
2. Eyelet and round hole punch and eyelet pliers for riveting
3. Leather edger tools
4. A die-cutting machine or embossing machine (such as a Sizzix®) with metal die cuts

For Painting, Decorating or Accessory Crafting

1. Sponges, brushes and fabric scraps
2. Bicomponent glue
3. Textile glue (we use Gütermann brand)
4. Silicone molds for resin
5. Looping and mandrel pliers for jewelry
6. Wire cutters

Techniques & Tricks

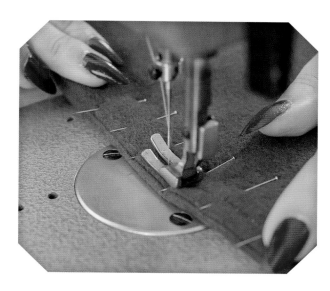

Sewing: French Seam Technique

A French seam encloses the seam edges on the inside of a sewn item so no raw edge is visible. This procedure eliminates the need for another form of finish. This works especially well for clothing if rough seams bother you. Once you understand the steps, a French seam is quick and easy to sew.

Sew the first seam: Pin the wrong sides of the fabric together where you want your seam to be so the seam allowance will be on the right side of the fabric. This is the opposite of how you would normally sew a seam. Sew the seam.

Press the seam: Press the seam as it was sewn. Then, fold the fabric along the seam line, so the right sides of the fabric are together and the stitching is at the edge of the fold. Press well, so you are working with a sharp crease at the fold on the seam.

Enclose the seam and press again: Press the second seam as it was sewn. Then, open the fabric with the wrong side facing up and press the seam to one side. Finally, flip the fabric over and press the seam again with the right side facing up.

Leather Tricks

Use neatsfoot oil for deep moisturizing and to add softness to the leather; apply when the piece is finished.

Use Tokonole, a Japanese product that is applied on the inner side of the leather to smooth the surface. It is essential for masks to make them more comfortable to wear.

Choose the right thickness of leather for the piece you are going to create. For example, to create masks or purses, the thickness should be between $1/16$ and $5/64$ inches (1.5 and 2 mm); for holsters or belts, the perfect leather thickness would be between $1/8$ and $9/64$ inches (3 and 3.5 mm).

Resins

Use lighters or a small blowtorch on the epoxy resin when it is already poured to eliminate bubbles. You can also spray it with alcohol, although it is less effective.

Remove the resin with silicone spatulas so that it releases fewer bubbles.

Sizing Your Sewing Patterns

Modifying the size of a sewing pattern is a common task for tailors and sewists who want to create garments that fit perfectly. Whether you need to make a pattern smaller or larger, the process involves a few simple steps. In this guide we will explore how to modify a sewing pattern.

Materials
- The sewing pattern you wish to modify
- Tracing paper or pattern paper
- Pencil or pen
- Ruler
- Scissors

Making the Pattern Smaller

1. Start by calculating the difference between the pattern's current size and your desired size.

2. Using a ruler, draw a vertical line on the pattern through the key points (such as the bust, waist or hip) that require modification.

3. Measure and mark the distance from the original pattern line to the desired smaller size, ensuring the reduction is evenly distributed.

4. Connect the marked points using a ruler, creating a rough outline of your new pattern line.

5. Repeat this process for all necessary key points on the pattern.

6. Once you have modified all the key points, use a ruler to draw new lines connecting the modified points, ensuring the lines are smooth and maintain the original shape of the pattern.

7. Cut out the modified pattern along the new lines, discarding the excess paper.

8. Transfer the modified pattern onto tracing paper or pattern paper, ensuring all markings and labels are clear.

Making the Pattern Larger

1. Start by calculating the difference between the pattern's current size and your desired size.

2. Draw a vertical line on the pattern through the key points that require modification.

3. Measure and mark the distance from the original pattern line to the desired larger size, distributing the enlargement evenly.

4. Connect the marked points using a ruler, creating a new pattern line.

5. Repeat this process for all necessary key points on the pattern.

6. Draw new lines connecting the modified points, maintaining the shape and proportions of the original pattern.

7. Cut out the modified pattern along the new lines.

8. Transfer the modified pattern onto tracing paper or pattern paper, ensuring all markings and labels are clear.

Note: Regardless of whether you are making the pattern smaller or larger, it's essential to double-check the modified pattern against your measurements and make any necessary adjustments before cutting and sewing the fabric. Remember to leave seam allowances as indicated on the original pattern or add them to the modified pattern.

By following these steps, you can easily modify the size of a sewing pattern to be smaller or larger. Remember to take accurate measurements, make even modifications and transfer the modified pattern onto a clean sheet of paper to ensure clarity and accuracy. With practice, you will gain confidence in modifying patterns and create garments that fit you perfectly. Happy sewing!

The Fairy

Get Inspired: Fairy Inspo

The earliest fairy stories date back to the Middle Ages, when fairies were described as protective beings. In the fifteenth century, they began to be portrayed in tales as small creatures that inhabit natural environments, but with a lot of mysticism surrounding them. It was not clear whether they were good or evil, so the tales would warn people to avoid places where fairies lived.

There is no evident origin, but the popular or folkloric beliefs of many different civilizations sometimes tell us stories with aspects in common. We like to think of fairies as nature spirits. The Celtic revival, or Irish Literary Revival, kept fairies part of the Celtic cultural heritage. In addition to their folkloric origins, they are often depicted in Renaissance literature and art, so we think they fit perfectly into a Renaissance faire.

We are inspired by butterfly species such as the monarch butterfly, the emperor moth or the luna moth because we consider them to be such gorgeous insects, with such intense colors and wonderful patterns on their wings that they have always looked to us like something out of a fairy tale. That's why our Elastic Halter Top (page 15) and Maxiskirt (page 17) resemble the wings of butterflies or moths.

Fairies are mostly depicted with wings, a human appearance and with magical powers. Many more recent illustrations portray them with butterfly or dragonfly wings, like our Butterfly Wings (page 21).

Elastic Halter Top

For the top of our fairy, inspired by the tales that imagine some fairies as creatures able to camouflage themselves as insects and other forest animals, we found inspiration for the print of the fabric in the wings of the monarch butterfly. You can use any printed fabric for this project, or see the Butterfly Wings section (page 21) for information on how to get custom fabrics.

Materials
- ½ yard (½ m) elastic fabric such as scuba or neoprene
- 2 yards (2 m) elastic strap (such as for swimsuits)

Tools
- Sewing machine
- Chalk or fabric marking pen

1. Turn to the project pattern on page i for this piece. Trace them onto paper and cut them out. Then trace the outline of the pattern pieces on the fabric with chalk or a fabric marking pen. With the right sides together, stitch the back pieces to the front piece along the edges, joining them with a simple stitch.

2. Along the edges of each curved section of the back pieces, make a zigzag edging stitch.

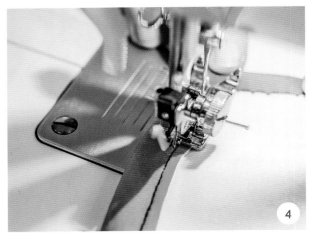

3. On both back pieces, fold the straight edges 1 to 2 inches (2.5 to 5 cm) over to the wrong side to create a loop for the strap, then sew using a narrow zigzag stitch.

4. Repeat step 3 along the neckline.

5. For the rest of the edges, hem with a zigzag stitch. (It is important to use a zigzag stitch to allow the pieces to stretch.)

6. Thread the strap through each loop as shown in the photo.

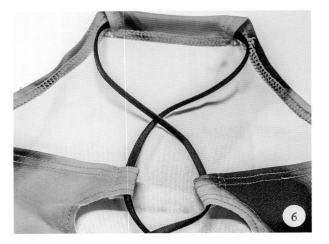

Maxiskirt

The print on the skirt of our fairy was also inspired by the texture and colors of the wings of the monarch butterfly—so our fairy will be able to camouflage as a butterfly. See the Butterfly Wings section (page 21) for information on how to get custom fabrics.

Materials
- 3 yards (3 m) printed chiffon or voile
- 3 yards (3 m) lining fabric if the skirt fabric is very sheer
- 1–2 yards (1–2 m) flat elastic ribbon about 1½" (4 cm) wide (we recommend a very flexible elastic for a more comfortable garment)

Tools
- Measuring tape
- Pins and chalk for marking fabric
- Sewing machine (we recommend an overlock machine)

1. Fold the fabric chosen for your skirt in half. Measure your waist circumference and add 8 inches (20 cm). Divide this number in half. Using the halved number, lay the measuring tape in an arc in the upper corner of the fabric. Mark this line with pins or chalk.

2. Measure the height between your belly button and the floor (or the spot where you want your skirt to end). This will be the length of the skirt.

3. With pins or chalk, mark the length of the skirt determined in step 2 in the bottom-right corner of the fabric square. Using chalk, trace an arc from the marked corner to the upper-left corner of the fabric square, sweeping the chalk like the hands of a clock. Cut the fabric along the marked curve for the waist marked in step 1 and the length.

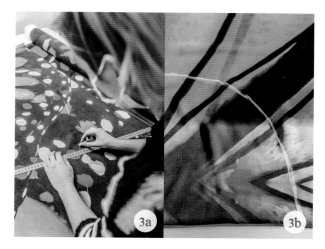

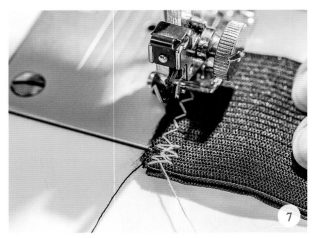

4. If the fabric chosen is very thin or sheer, repeat steps 1–3 with the lining fabric.

5. Measure your waist circumference and subtract ¾ to 1½ inches (2 to 4 cm) from it; use the resulting number to cut the flat elastic ribbon for the waistband.

6. Close the skirt down the back seam so that the cut piece forms a shape that would be almost a circle. If the fabric is very thin, we recommend sewing this seam using an overlock stitch. Also use overlock or zigzag stitches at the bottom edge.

7. Sew the two ends of the elastic waistband together with several tight stitches.

8. To attach the skirt to the waistband, stretch the elastic band while you sew so that the chiffon of the skirt then gathers when the elastic is in its relaxed state, allowing the skirt to be very full.

9. If you want the waistband seam to be more concealed and you have lined the skirt, place the waistband between the outer fabric (placed on top) and the lining (placed underneath) while joining the three pieces at the same time (while stretching the elastic band as described in step 8).

Our fairy now has a skirt made of butterfly wings! This same ethereal, airy and spring or summery garment can be very different if you make it in other fabrics or colors. If you do use a different fabric, make sure the fabric you choose is not too thick to be attached to the elastic waistband.

Butterfly Wings

The vision of the fairy with wings is a classic that appears in many traditional fairy-tale illustrations. There are countless types of wings shown on fairy beings: butterfly wings, moth wings, dragonfly wings, bird wings or even angel wings. So, design your fairy wings in any way you would like!

In this project we will make monarch butterfly wings, resulting in a flower-dwelling fairy that camouflages itself with the insects of the forest to deceive the unbelieving eye.

Our butterfly wings are made of fabric printed with the image of monarch wings. You can have your fabric printed on the Spoonflower website (www.spoonflower.com) or similar dye sublimation websites. You can also create an image yourself from a drawing of butterflies but remember that the print will need to be very large (see materials list for size). We recommend using a lightweight fabric such as chiffon because the wings are somewhat transparent and should have color on both sides (a thicker fabric will be white on one side).

Materials
- 51 x 114" (130 x 290 cm) printed chiffon voile fabric
- 2 yards (2 m) black satin bias binding, ¾" (2 cm) wide
- 2 (1-yard [1-m]) black satin ribbons, ½" (1.3 cm) wide
- 2 (35" [90-cm]) pieces of galvanized wire (can be found in garden supply stores) or wire coated with silicone or rubber

Tools
- Wire cutters
- Needles for hand-sewing
- Sewing machine

1. Cut the printed fabric following the outline of the wing, leaving an outside margin of ¼ inch (6 mm). Try to make the cut as rounded and smooth as possible, without sharp angles, peaks or inlets. This will make sewing easier.

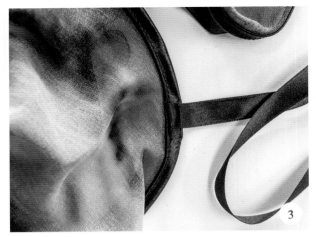

2. Sew the bias binding along the entire length of the butterfly wing margin. To do this, open the bias binding, place the wing on top, with its margin in the middle of the open bias binding, and fold to the left to trap the printed fabric inside the bias binding. Sew it closed with a simple seam about $\frac{1}{16}$ inch (2 mm) from the bias binding margin.

3. Continue sewing the bias binding all the way around the butterfly wing. Then find the center of the top of the wing, as this is where the neckline will be. Mark 8 inches (20 cm) on each side of the center and sew two 1-yard (1-m)-long satin ribbons at these two points. You will use these ribbons to close the wings like a cape.

4. At the bottom of each wing, make a small opening in the bias binding or in the seam that closes the bias binding.

5. Into one of the holes, insert one piece of the galvanized (or coated wire) and push the wire through the outer edge of the wing inside the bias tape channel. Repeat on the other side.

6. Close the two openings with a hand stitch so that the wire does not slip out and the bias stitching cannot unravel.

   And that is it! Your fairy being is ready to spread its wings and fly through the forest.

⊱ Leaf Mask ⊰

In this project we are going to create a fairy mask with the shape of a realistic leaf, perfect to hide your identity when attending a magical ball or to complement your outdoor outfit to allow you to be one with the forest. We chose for our fairy character a shade of brown that goes with the tones of autumn and tree logs and matches the other items of our fairy's outfit. Although our fairy belongs to the autumn court, you can use leather of other colors or undyed leather to create the tones you want.

Materials
- 1 (8" [20-cm]) sheet of brown leather, ⅛" (3 mm) thick
- Leather dye (we used Pro Dye in dark brown and black)
- 2 (12" [30-cm]) ribbons, ½" (1.3 cm) wide
- Contact glue
- 2 (⅜–¾" [1–2 cm]) metal rings

Tools
- Marker, pen or pencil
- Leather cutter or scalpel
- Awl or beveler leather tool for texturing
- Brush to apply the dye and glue
- Sponge or a piece of cotton or wool fabric to blend the dye
- Foam mannequin head

1. Turn to the project pattern on page i for this piece. Trace it onto paper and cut it out. Trace the pattern on the leather using a marker, pen or pencil.

2. Using a leather cutter or scalpel, cut around the outer margin of the piece and cut out the holes for the eyes.

3. Make very superficial cuts, without going through the thickness of the leather, to depict the veins of the leaf.

4. Deepen the surface cuts in the veins by exerting pressure with an awl to open them and give depth to the markings.

5. Paint the vein lines with the dark brown leather dye using a brush. Work as quickly as possible to avoid leaving brushstrokes visible. You can also tint more easily with a larger sponge to cover more surface area without leaving brush lines, but you will waste more dye this way.

6. Paint the outer edges of the mask with a brush and the black dye.

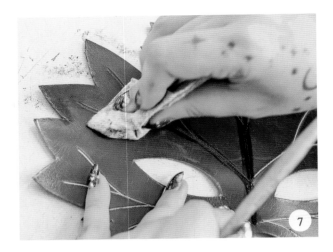

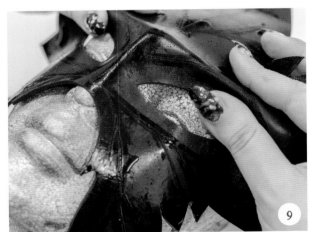

7. With a sponge or piece of cotton or wool fabric, blend the dye strokes.

8. Allow the dye to air-dry and then briefly soak the entire mask in water until it is moistened.

9. Using a foam mannequin head, apply pressure with your fingers to mold the moistened mask to the shape of the face so that it acquires three-dimensionality and conforms to the face.

10. Twist the tips of the leaves by turning or pinching them to make them look more realistic.

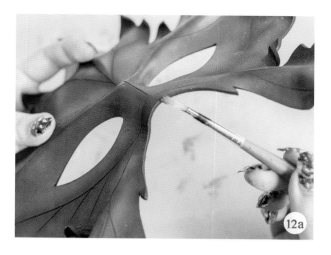

11. Let the mask dry on the mannequin.

12. When the mask is completely dry, paint the outer margins and the edge of the opening for the eyes with black leather dye.

13. Finally, cut two pieces off one of the ribbons, each piece about 3 inches (8 cm) long. Glue the end of one ribbon to the inside of the mask, between the outside of the eyes and the edge of the mask. Thread one of the metal rings onto the ribbon. Then fold the ribbon over the ring and glue it down, to trap the ring. Repeat this on the opposite eye with the other 3-inch (8-cm) ribbon. Thread the 12-inch (30-cm) ribbon through the rings and use it to tie the mask to your head.

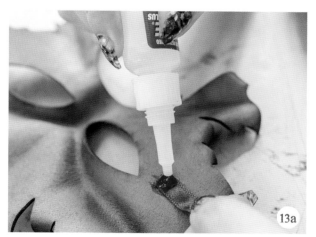

Put It All Together

Hair, Makeup and Other Accessories

When we design characters from imagination, from legends and fairy tales, we allow ourselves much more license and free rein. You can be as fanciful in makeup and hairstyle as you want, using as many fantasy elements as you can think of, such as crystals, iridescent shadows, glitter and so on.

Here is a makeup trick! Use temporary butterfly tattoos split in half to add wings to the corners of your eyes.

Use mascara in shades that match and complement the rest of your look.

Add themed jewelry, bracelets, bangles, chokers and earrings, with natural shapes, leaves, branches or insects.

Decorate your hair with metal flowers and jewelry, beads, pearls or crystal chains.

The Peasant

Get Inspired: From the Woods and Cottagecore to Hobbiton

The peasant look is one of the most common at Renaissance faires, because historically these were the outfits most often seen on villagers and country folk, usually when they visited markets to stock up or sell their own wares.

The peasant is a very versatile character that allows many combinations and additions of elements such as overskirts and accessories hanging from the belt and aprons, all depending on the look you want to achieve. Also, due to the comfort of this outfit and its relative ease of tailoring, it is very common among today's Renaissance faire market vendors and for the more casual attendees, making it an ideal choice for attending such fairs for the first time.

With the popularization of the cottagecore style, the usual villager garments have become much more fashionable, often with fancy additions. The cottagecore aesthetic has a predominant palette of tones, textures and elements that romanticize rural and rugged living, a simple life in harmony with nature. It is a continuation of other aesthetics but comes from Romanticism and the Victorian era transposed to the English countryside.

The Arts and Crafts movement is also a great inspiration for attire of this type, especially for the floral patterns usually used in this aesthetic.

The peasant look is also influenced in many cases by fairy fantasy literature and medieval and Renaissance books such as Tolkien's *The Lord of the Rings* and other English fairy tales, so hobbit-like peasant garb would also be an ideal character for this look.

Chemise Underdress

This underdress is an essential garment of Renaissance attire, which you can combine with an infinite number of accessories, belts, bodices, overskirts, aprons and so on.

Materials
- 3 yards (3 m) viscose fabric
- 3 yards (3 m) flat elastic band, ⅜" (1 cm) wide

Tools
- Chalk to mark the fabric
- Scissors
- Needles
- Pins
- Thread
- Measuring tape
- Larger needle with ¾" (2-cm) eye or a 1–2" (2.5–5-cm) safety pin

1. Turn to the project patterns on pages ii–vii for this piece. Trace it onto paper and cut it out. Draw the patterns on the fabric, cut them out and join the front and back pieces with regular seams. When cutting the fabric, if you notice the fibers tend to open and fray, go over the edge of the seam with a zigzag or overlock stitch.

2. Close the seams on both sleeves and join the sleeves to the body.

3. Make a hem stitch at the neckline a little more than ³⁄₈ inch (1 cm) wide so that the flat elastic band will be able to pass through. At the end of this hem stitch, leave a small section open so that you can insert the flat elastic band that will gather the neckline of the chemise.

4. Measure the distance of the outer edges of your shoulders and multiply by two. Use this measurement to cut the flat elastic band to size. After it is cut, pass it through the opening left in step 3. Use the large needle or a safety pin to thread the elastic through the neckline and back out the same hole it entered.

5. Sew the ends of the elastic together with several stitches. When you release the elastic, it will gather the upper part of the neckline and the shoulders of the garment. Using a simple stitch, close the hole where you inserted the elastic.

6. Repeat steps 3–5 to create the ruffles at the ends of both sleeves, using the circumference of your arm just above the elbow to measure and cut two pieces of flat elastic band.

7. To finish the bottom edge of the dress, use a hem stitch, a zigzag or overlock stitch.

❧ Renaissance Bodice ❧

Lace-up bodices and vests are one of the most common Renaissance peasant-style garments; however, they are often made of fabrics that only nobles and royals could actually afford. For a more historical look for lower-class peasants, use coarser fabrics that were more common and more readily available, such as linen, cotton or flax.

Inspired by a Romantic–Renaissance period piece, our printed bodice uses two layers of beautiful, breathable fabric and is made for comfort without boning. You can wear this bodice completely laced closed or lace it looser to remain partially open. The front and back lacings can be cinched perfectly to your preference. Wear it over any Middle Ages dress or Renaissance chemise, such as the Chemise Underdress on page 33.

Materials
- ½ yard (½ m) printed canvas fabric for the exterior
- ½ yard (½ m) canvas fabric for the lining
- 4 yards (3.6 m) suede, cotton or velvet bias tape, 1¼" (3 cm) wide
- 24 pairs (¼" [6-mm]) eyelet rivets
- 7 yards (7 m) satin ribbon, ½" (1.3 cm) wide

Tools
- Scissors
- Pins
- Needle
- Thread
- Eyelet hole punch and riveter
- Chalk or fabric marking pen

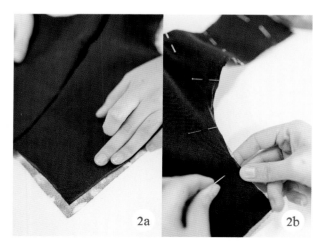

1. Turn to the project patterns on pages i–iii for this piece. Trace them onto paper and cut them out. Then trace the outline of the pattern pieces on the fabric with chalk or a fabric marking pen. Cut out all the bodice pieces in the exterior fabric. After that, cut out all the bodice pieces in the lining fabric. Join the shoulder and side seams of exterior pieces. Also join the shoulder and side seams of the lining fabric.

2. Pin the exterior and lining fabric together with the wrong (seamed sides) together. The exterior (non-seamed side) of both pieces should be visible.

3. Baste the pieces close to the edge to make them easier to handle.

4. Sew the bias tape around all the edges of the bodice and around the armholes.

5. Along both sides of the front closure, use an eyelet hole punch to make holes through the exterior and lining every 1¼ inches (3 cm).

6. Rivet the holes with the metal eyelets.

7. Thread the satin ribbon through the eyelets to be able to adjust the bodice.

And that is it! Now you have a garment that will give an authentic touch to your Renaissance outfit. You can make bodices with different seasonal prints to attend different themed fairs throughout the year.

Ivy Crown & Hair Pins

In this project you will create some hair accessories that can be made with elements found in nature such as leaves, branches, fallen fruits or flowers. You can also use fabric or plastic versions so they can be worn multiple times.

The crown we chose for this project can be an ideal complement to attend a Ren faire at any time of the year. You can create multiple crowns using different elements to be worn according to the season.

Materials
- 21" (55 cm) raffia-covered thick wire
- Ivy branches, either natural and dried or artificial
- Thin dark green or brown floral wire
- 1 yard (1 m) satin, organza, velvet or rope ribbon
- Hairpins or bobby pins
- Textile glue (we use Gütermann brand)

Tools
- Tape measure
- Wire cutters or jewelers' pliers for cutting and bending wire

1. Measure the circumference of your head. With wire cutters or jewelers' pliers, cut the raffia-covered wire to that size.

2. Using jewelers' pliers, turn the ends of the wire back on themselves to create an eyelet at each end, then wrap the end several times to close the loops. You will use the loops to adjust the crown to your head.

3. Attach strips of ivy branches or any other flexible branches with leaves or flowers to the raffia-covered wire using floral wire.

4. Pass a ribbon through the two eyelets at both ends of the raffia-covered wire to adjust the crown.

5. To make the hair pins, select pairs of leaves as small as you can find and that are of similar size and shape.

6. Using textile glue, attach each leaf to a hairpin or bobby pin.

7. Glue the other leaf of the pair on the other side of the hairpin or bobby pin, making a "sandwich." Allow the glue to dry completely.

And that's it! Now you have a flexible, lightweight, comfortable and durable set of accessories to complete many types of outfits, not just the peasant's, as you will discover as you go through the projects in this book. Remember that you can use other types of branches or even add decorations, such as replicas of mushrooms, pine cones, acorns, etc., to give the headdress a whole new style.

Put It All Together

Hair, Makeup and Other Accessories

Complete your garb with elements reminiscent of the countryside, country life or Hobbiton, such as baskets, bags to hang on your belt, sacks or even items to match your character such as old keys or craft tools. You can add hats or scarves to cover your hair. Flower crowns are also very common in Ren faires. Don't hesitate to add several layers of clothing such as overskirts, shawls and so on.

For hair, we recommend curling it or braiding it into a crown in which you can intersperse leaves, flowers or even miniature mushroom replicas.

Keep your eye makeup earth-toned, then add plenty of blush to your cheeks, nose and chin. Perhaps add golden shading, as if your skin has been tanned in the sun.

The Hunter

Get Inspired: Human or Elf?

The hunter is a classic Ren faire archetype, so we will make several
elements that might help you create this character. All the items you will
learn to create through these projects can completely change the look of
the hunter if you use different fabrics or colors.

Whether you want to be Snow White's huntsman, a mountain ranger
or a forest elf, all these use the same patterns and processes. Just add
accessories such as a bow, crossbow or daggers to give the final touch that
will add personality to your look.

For a more historical or human look, choose materials such as linen and
wool in natural colors such as brown, beige or khaki. If you are looking for
a more fantasy or elven look, you can use velvets, silks or even linen, and
go for grays, greens and metallic tones.

You could even transform your look into a rogue using dark colors to help
you go unnoticed. This look is completely unisex and all the garments and
pieces can be adapted to any size.

Don't keep it simple: Add as many bags, belts, weapons and accessories as
you would like!

Hooded Wool Capelet

In this project you will create a hunter's wool capelet, a short cape with a hood to cover the shoulders and complement your outdoor outfit. The capelet will keep you warm and comfortable while you are exploring autumn or winter woods and will keep you camouflaged among the forest vegetation. We chose, for the styling of this hunting character, a shade of green that is in tune with the tones of nature, tree leaves, moss and other natural elements.

Although this design might look simple for a druid or medieval peasant outfit, you can add extra decorations to your cape such as lace, fur fabric or plain or embroidered ribbons along the edges. Choose a closure for the cape fastening depending on the style or aesthetic (Celtic, medieval, cottagecore) you want for your garment or depending on the type of fabric chosen (satin, rustic, etc.). Embroidered, satin, printed or damask fabrics look better with metallic closures in curved and elegant finishes, while more rustic fabrics such as wool, canvas, suede or linen would look better with simple closures.

Materials
* 80" (2 m) wool, velvet, twill, jacquard or other fabric with weight and drape
* Closures of your choice

Tools
* Iron
* Chalk or fabric marking pen
* Scissors
* Pins
* Thread
* Sewing machine (overlock if possible)

1. Lay out the fabric and fold it in half. The folded margin of the fabric will be the center of the back of the cape; there will be no seam on the back. Make sure the fabric does not have any wrinkles. If it does, iron the fabric before proceeding.

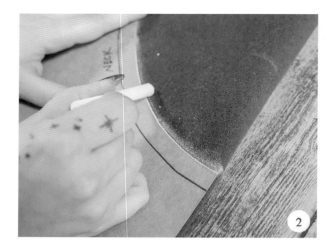

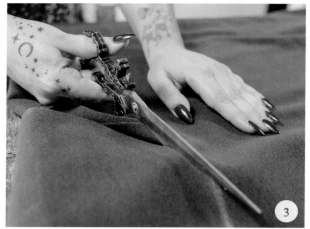

2. Turn to the project patterns on pages iii–vi for this piece. Trace them onto paper and cut them out. Trace the outline of the pattern on the fabric with chalk or a fabric marking pen.

3. Cut out all pieces of the fabric inside the marks you have drawn, so that the chalk marks are on the discarded piece of fabric. Try not to move the fabric while cutting to prevent it from slipping and having an irregular or asymmetrical cut.

4. Pin the hood to the body of the cape. Add pins perpendicular to the outer margin of the fabric to join the cut pieces, always with the pointed part of the pin toward the edge of the fabric, to be able to pass the sewing machine over them without having to remove them while sewing.

5. Sew the two pieces of the hood together, then sew the hood to the body of the cape using French seams (see page 9 in Techniques & Tricks).

6. Iron the seam open to make it easier to handle and complete the next step of the French seam method. Do not skip this step; ironing the seams (and in some cases the fabric before cutting) is essential!

7. Face the opposite sides of the fabric to catch the previous seam allowance with a new seam. The open seam becomes the new margin. Place pins perpendicular to the end and with the pin points toward the edge of the fabric, so that you can pass over the seam with the sewing machine without removing the pins.

8. Sew this folded side with a ⅜-inch (1-cm) margin to ensure that the seam margin from the previous step does not poke out. It is important that the seams in this method are made as straight and parallel as possible.

9. Finish off the outer edge of the bottom of the garment with a narrow overlock seam or with a zigzag seam if you don't have an overlock sewing machine. This type of finish ensures a clean and fine outer edge that does not affect the drape of the fabric.

10. Hand sew a single hem seam along the entire front of the garment through the chest and hood. It is important that the fold and seam are very straight and parallel so that this hem does not have wrinkles or look uneven. For fabrics with a fiber that easily detaches from the weave, use an overlock seam before hemming so that the fabric does not unravel. Remember to iron the seam after sewing this front finish.

11. Sew the closure by hand so that the thread is as invisible or concealed as possible, sliding the needle under the closure and choosing a thread color that is a close match to the fabric.

Now your capelet is complete! To find other inspirations to complete your look beyond the other hunter's projects, see the Creating Your Own Character section on page 112.

Medieval Linen Shirt

The garment you will learn to make in this project is a key element for many medieval or Renaissance-inspired outfits. Our shirt pattern adapts to anyone, it is very easy to scale the sizes and it can work with all the characters that appear in this book, so we hope you try making this shirt with other fabrics and colors to get the most out of this pattern.

Materials
- 2 yards (2 m) linen, cotton or similar fabric
- ½ yard (½ m) cotton bias binding that matches the fabric
- 30 x 50" (76 x 127 cm) adhesive interfacing (optional)
- 18 pairs eyelet rivets
- ½ yard (½ m) twine, cord, ribbon or string that matches your fabric

Tools
- Chalk or fabric marking pen
- Scissors
- Sewing machine
- Pins
- Iron
- Eyelet hole punch
- Hand or table riveting machine

1. Turn to the project patterns on pages i-iii and v for this piece. Trace them onto paper and cut them out. Then trace the outline of the pattern pieces on the fabric with chalk or a fabric marking pen. Cut out all the pattern pieces. Sew the seams on both sleeves. Sew the two side seams of the lower torso. Join the seam of each sleeve to the two side seams of the lower torso. Join the two shoulder seams.

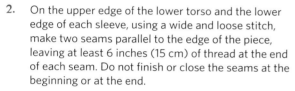

2. On the upper edge of the lower torso and the lower edge of each sleeve, using a wide and loose stitch, make two seams parallel to the edge of the piece, leaving at least 6 inches (15 cm) of thread at the end of each seam. Do not finish or close the seams at the beginning or at the end.

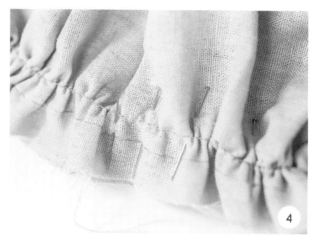

3. Pull the threads left at the end of the lower torso seams to gather or ruffle the fabric until its size matches the size of the upper torso piece.

4. Distribute and fix the ruffles by placing pins every few inches (or centimeters) to make sure the ruffles are evenly distributed and do not move.

5. Match the size of the ruffled piece to the lower torso again to double-check that the pieces match. Then, sew a line of stitching to secure the ruffles while removing the pins. Sew the ruffled edge of the lower torso to the bottom edge of the upper torso.

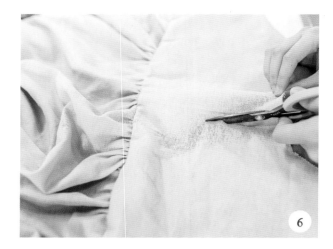

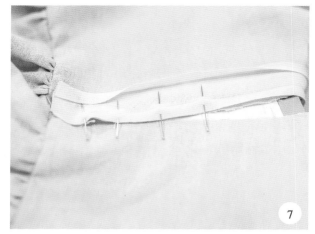

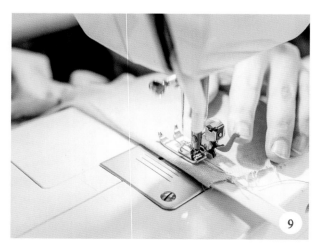

6. In the center of the front piece of the upper torso, make a perpendicular cut from the neckline (marked on the pattern).

7. Place one open piece of the cotton bias binding along the edge of one side of the cut neckline of the shirt, leaving ⅜ inch (1 cm) of bias binding at the top and bottom of the piece. Pin the bias binding to the fabric and stitch.

8. Along the seam, fold the bias binding toward the inside of the piece.

9. Sew a topstitch to fix the fold. This will create a neckline with a simple but effective and solid surface for piercing and riveting later. Cut the excess bias binding at the top and bottom of the piece.

10. Repeat steps 7–9 on the other side of the neckline.

11

12

11. If you want a thicker and stiffer collar and cuffs, add interfacing to the collar and cuff pieces. We recommend using adhesive interfacing that you can cut and iron to the fabric very easily.

12. To make the seam of the cuffs and collar neat, first make a fold toward the inside of the two pieces before sewing the seam (they are all double pieces).

13. Fix these folds with pins and iron carefully, so that the fold will be easier to sew. Join the two collar pieces and the sleeve cuff pieces.

13

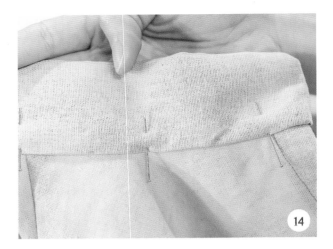

14. Join the neckline of the upper torso piece to the collar with a simple stitch.

15. Pull the threads left at the end of the sleeve seams to gather or ruffle the fabric until its size matches the size of the cuffs. Distribute and fix the ruffles by placing pins every few inches (or centimeters) to make sure the ruffles are evenly distributed and do not move, then sew a simple line of stitches to fix the ruffles in place. Attach the sleeve ruffles to the cuffs.

16. Using an eyelet hole punch, make holes along the neckline approximately 1 inch (2.5 cm) apart.

17. Add metal eyelet rivets to each hole.

18. Using an eyelet hole punch, make two holes on each side of the ends of each sleeve cuff and rivet them as well.

19. Thread twine, cord, ribbon or string through the eyelets along the neckline and each sleeve.

Now you have a must-have garment! Remember to try making this shirt in different fabrics. You can also try changing the volume or length of the pieces to have puffier sleeves or a garment that looks more like a tunic by changing the length of the lower torso piece. Experiment with the pattern and see how your changes affect the final piece.

～ Leather Belt ～

Our hunter needs some accessories for his outfit, to carry his weapons, bags, or to hang or set his traps. Therefore, in this project you will learn how to make a handmade belt. As with the rest of the projects in this book, you will be able to modify the materials used to obtain other accessories following the same steps but by changing the shape or color.

Materials
- Leather strip, cut at the width of your belt buckle, and at the length of your hip circumference plus 4" (10 cm)
- Leather dye (we used brown Pro Dye)
- Metal buckle
- 1 pair flat metal rivets

Tools
- Paper and fabric die-cutting machine (we use a Sizzix) and metal dies with motif or texture, or leather die cut and hammer
- Sponge or fabric scraps for dyeing
- Eyelet hole punch
- Pencil or fabric marker
- Hand or table riveting machine

1. Engrave your desired texture on the leather strip with a die-cutting machine or with leather die cuts and a hammer. If using the die-cutting machine, first wet the leather slightly (it should be damp, not soaking wet). Place the metal die with the desired texture on the leather strip and pass it through the die-cutting machine at least twice to mark the leather well (these machines are designed for paper or thin fabric, so it may need a second pass to mark a thicker material).

2. Dye the leather strip with a sponge and brown dye (or the color of your choice). Allow the leather to dry completely.

3. Place the buckle on the leather strip to mark the exit hole of the moving part of the buckle and punch a hole in the center of the leather strip at the height delimited by your buckle.

4. Mark the center of the opposite end of the strip. With an eyelet hole punch, punch a hole in the center of the width.

5. Fold the marked end of the strip over and insert a pencil or marker through the hole created in step 5 and mark the hole. Using an eyelet hole punch, punch a hole through the leather strip through the mark.

6. Thread the buckle onto the leather strip, fold it over and using a hand or table riveting machine, rivet the two ends of the leather strip together.

7. On the other end of the belt strip, make several equidistant holes in the center of the strip to allow you to adjust the size of the belt if you want to wear it higher or lower on your hip.

Belt Pouch

In this project you will learn how to make a handmade belt pouch with leather and fabric scraps. Feel free to modify the materials used to make different versions of this pouch for other characters. Remember that the limit is your imagination. You can completely change the look of your purse by changing the fabric (instead of wool, you can use scraps of linen, velvet, etc. from any of the other projects in this book) or you can also change the pattern on the leather by buying other shapes of cutting dies or drawing yourself anything on a small piece of leather.

Materials
- Square scrap of leather for the top of the pouch, approximately 4" (10 cm)
- Square scrap of fabric remnant (such as from the Hooded Wool Capelet [page 47]), approximately 8" (20 cm)
- Leather dye (we used brown Pro Dye)
- Fine-tipped gold gel marker
- 28 pairs metal eyelets
- 2 pairs flat metal rivets
- ½ yard (½ m) rope, ribbon or suede string
- 1 stud metal rivet higher than the thickness of your leather scrap

Tools
- Scissors and leather cutter
- Paper and fabric die-cutting machine (we use a Sizzix) and metal dies with motif or texture
- Sponge or fabric scraps for dyeing
- Eyelet hole punch
- Chalk for marking fabric
- Hand or table riveting machine

3

1. Turn to the project pattern on page viii for this piece. Trace and cut out the pattern for the leather cover from your leather scrap.

2. Lightly moisten the leather piece; it does not need to be very wet.

3. Mark the leather cover, while slightly damp, with the blade die of your choice. Place the die and the leather piece in the die-cutting machine and run it through the machine. If you can't find a die you like, or don't have access to a die-cutting machine, you can draw a design on the leather.

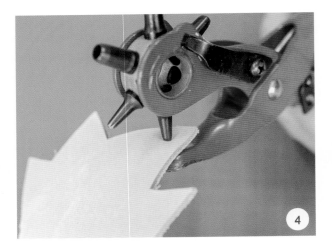

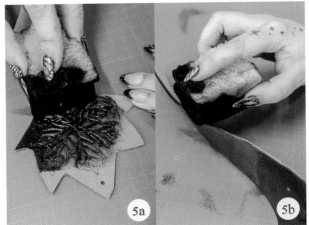

4. Mark the three circles indicated by the pattern on the leather, then use an eyelet hole punch to punch them out.

5. Dye the top and sides of the leather pouch cover with a sponge. Allow the leather to dry completely.

6. Trace the die-cut pattern in the leather pouch cover using the gold marker.

7. Fold the fabric and place the straight line of the pattern on the fold of the fabric. Using chalk or a marker, trace the pattern onto the fabric. Also mark all the circles for the holes and rivets. Cut out the fabric pouch.

8. Use an eyelet hole punch to make all the holes shown on the pattern.

9. Rivet eyelets into all the marked holes in the fabric pouch except for two adjoining holes. Leave two adjoining holes empty.

10. To join the leather cover to the fabric pouch with the two flat metal rivets, put the rivets through the holes in the leather cover, then through the two adjoining empty holes in the fabric you left in step 9. Loop the long end of the leather cover around the fabric then rivet the three layers together, trapping the fabric between the two pieces of leather.

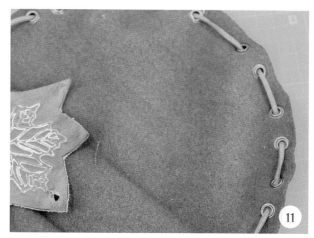

11. Thread a string through the remaining pouch eyelet holes starting at the right-hand eyelet of the pair of holes closest to the stud metal rivet. Thread all the way around the pouch and end at the left-hand eyelet hole closest to the stud metal rivet. Tie a knot at both ends of the string so it does not come loose.

12. Pull the ends of the strings to close the pouch and create your bag. Close the leather cover over the pouch. Insert a marker through the hole in the leather cover, to mark the location for the stud rivet on the pouch. Use an eyelet hole punch to make a hole in the fabric. Then, use a hand or table riveting machine to insert the stud metal rivet in the hole in the fabric pouch.

And that's it! You can easily change the size of this pouch to carry other things. Try changing the lid by using other shapes and colors.

Elven Hair Barrette

In this tutorial you will learn to make a hair accessory that can be used for many different outfits depending on the shape, paint finishes and textures you choose. This tutorial shows how to make a barrette with molded leather and hand painting that would fit very well in the outfit of your hunter, being a human one or an elf explorer.

It is not necessary to have a specific pattern in this project, but if you want one, please refer to the pattern on page iv. Otherwise, you can find a real-life leaf to use as a reference. If your hair is thin or short, choose a narrow leaf (like an oak leaf) and if you have thicker, longer or braided hair, or hair with dreadlocks or curls, we recommend using a larger leaf (like the maple leaf).

Materials
- Leaf of your choice
- Scrap of natural-colored leather, $\frac{1}{16}$–$\frac{1}{8}$" (2–3 mm) thick and large enough to trace your leaf
- Leather dye (we used Pro Dye in green and yellow, or use colors of your choice; see step 5)
- Wooden or metal stick approximately 6" (15 cm) long and $\frac{1}{4}$" (6 mm) thick (find at beauty supply store or online)

Tools
- Pencil or pen
- Leather cutter or scalpel
- Dye cloth or sponge
- Awl leather tool
- Eyelet hole punch

1. Trace the outline of the leaf and its veins on the leather with a pencil or pen.

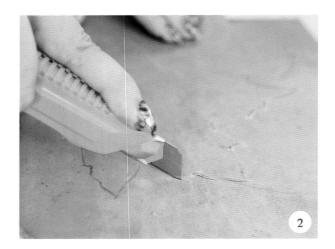

2. Cut out the leaf with a leather cutter or scalpel.

3. Dye the leather using a dye cloth or sponge. (We used a mixture of Pro Dye green and yellow to create a natural-looking shade.) Let the leather dry completely.

4. Mark the veins of the leaf with an awl tool that removes a very thin surface layer of leather.

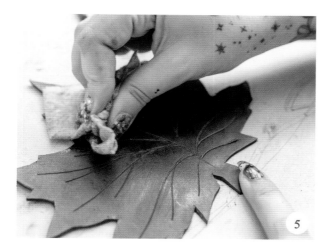

5

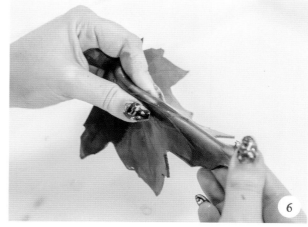

6

7

5. On the lines you marked with the awl, add more dye to darken the veins. It can be in the same tone, or you can use darker green, yellow, red or a color of your choice. Allow the dye to dry completely.

6. Moisten the leaf and shape it with your hands to give it three-dimensionality. If you have a lot of hair or very thick hair, create more of a curve so it will be able to contain more hair. Let the leather dry completely.

7. On either side of the leaf, using an eyelet hole punch, make two holes of the same diameter as the wooden or metal stick you have chosen.

And now you have an elven barrette! You can use this same technique with other leaves that you find in the forest and dye them so that they look like they have been collected at other times or seasons of the year, such as using yellow, reddish or brownish tones for fall. You could also draw any other shape on the leather to make pins for other outfits—there is a whole world of possibilities for long-haired elves!

Put It All Together

Hair, Makeup and Other Accessories

Choose the weapon that completes your outfit according to the type of hunter you want to be: elven daggers, crossbows or bows. Hang a holster from your belt to carry all your weapons or any other item that may be useful.

If you have long hair, braid it in a Viking or elvish style.

The more pouches or gadgets hanging from your belt, the better! You can even add several belts of different thicknesses or colors.

We recommend wearing rustic footwear with leather or braided knee-high boots. Try to avoid rubber soles, which would not have been available in the medieval period.

The Princess

Get Inspired: Choose Your Kingdom

The pre-Raphaelite vision of the Middle Ages is one of our main inspirations. In fact, we recommend you look for pre-Raphaelite paintings for inspiration. The main dress of this noble character is very much inspired by this look.

In the next set of projects, you can create a medieval princess in red velvet that will transport your mind to folk tales such as the Arthurian legends.

But if you chose other color combinations, such as blues and golds, you could look like a princess from a French court, or green tones and jewels with plant motifs to make you look like a princess that could have come straight out of Sherwood Forest. Add some pointed ears to your outfit and you can be the perfect elven princess.

Braid your hair to give it a more Targaryen look or leave it loose and wavy and combine it with white tones reminiscent of Galadriel. Don't forget to add as many accessories as you can to your outfit. In the Put It All Together section (page 86), you will find some inspirations to complete your styling.

Velvet Royal Dress

With the following tutorial we will make the most spectacular garment of the court, the princess dress. We have chosen a velvet in a burgundy color that transports us to the days of the Arthurian legends with characters like Guinevere, or pre-Raphaelite works such as those of John William Waterhouse.

By changing only the color of the fabric, but with different hair and jewelry accessories, you can place your costume in completely different worlds.

The sleeves have an open seam that runs the length of your arm. Using hooked clasps, you can close the sleeves or let them fall open.

Materials
- 5 yards (4.6 m) stretch velvet
- 6 pairs hooked clasps, approximately 1" (2.5 cm)

Tools
- Scissors
- Chalk or fabric marking pen
- Thread
- Sewing machine (overlock if possible)

1. Turn to the project patterns on pages iv–viii for this piece. Trace them onto paper and cut them out. Then trace the outline of the pattern pieces on the fabric with chalk or a fabric marking pen. Join the front and back pieces with a simple stitch, first at the shoulders and then down the sides. You can use zigzag or overlock on the edges of these seams.

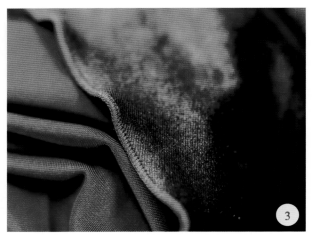

2. Attach the sleeves to the dress, using French seams (see the Techniques & Tricks section on page 9), making sure the sleeve opening is aligned at the top center of the shoulder.

3. Edge the hem of the dress and sleeves using a zigzag or overlock stitch. Also edge both sides of the sleeves using a zigzag or overlock stitch.

4. Along the neckline, make a thin but simple hemming stitch to avoid curls in the velvet fabric.

5. Hand sew three pairs of metal clasps on each sleeve, placing them 6 inches (15 cm) apart. This will allow you to open or close the sleeves.

And now you have a majestic Arthurian or elvish princess or queen dress! Remember that the accessories are essential as—or more important than—the choice of fabrics and colors to the final result.

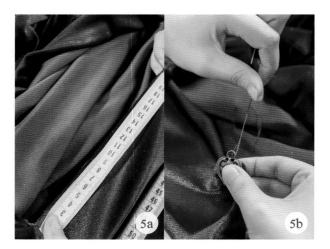

❧ Medieval Trim Belt ❧

Even if the fabric you choose for your princess dress is very nice in color, texture or richness, medieval dresses are usually very straight; therefore, a belt is a simple aesthetic option to enhance your waist, allowing you to adjust the dress without having to make it very tight.

For this tutorial we have chosen a golden metallic trim with burgundy decorations to match the rest of the gold accessories and the burgundy dress of our princess. You can find trim in many metallic shades, with or without embroidery, or of any style you feel will complement your look.

Materials
- 1½ yards (1½ m) trim or embroidered ribbon of your choice
- 8 eyelet rivets
- 2–3 yards (2–3 m) cord or ribbon for the belt closure

Tools
- Scissors
- Thread
- Pins
- Needle or sewing machine
- Measuring tape
- Eyelet hole punch
- Hand or table riveter

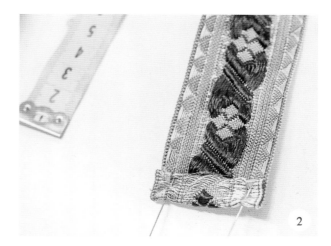

1. Cut two pieces of the trim (or embroidered ribbon): One should be 1 yard (1 m) long and another should be the circumference of your waist.

2. Make a ⅜-inch (1-cm) fold at both ends of the waistband strip. Secure with pins and stitch by hand or machine.

3. In the center of the waistband, fold the waistband to make a V shape and stitch to secure.

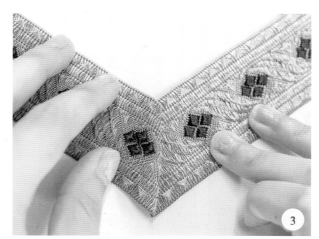

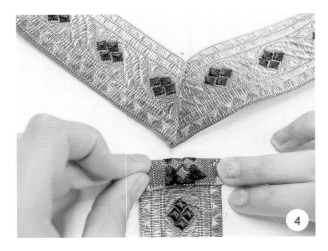

4. On the 1-yard (1-m) strip, make a ³⁄₈-inch (1-cm) fold at both ends. Secure with pins and stitch by hand or machine.

5. Join the 1-yard (1-m) strip perpendicular to the waist-band strip, behind the V-shaped peak in the center of the piece. Pin and sew both pieces together by hand or machine.

6. At the ends of the waistband, using an eyelet hole punch, make two holes at each end.

7. Finish the holes by sewing them as an eyelet with needle and thread or add rivets.

8. Thread a cord or ribbon through the eyelets as desired.

And now you have a nice belt that helps to stylize and complete your outfit. Make more than one belt so you can change your look each time you wear your dress.

Crown & Necklace

There is no proper princess without a castle or without a crown. Through this project you will learn a technique that will allow you to make many types of crowns or tiaras with resin in which you can encapsulate flowers, metal pieces or many other decorations. You can also make a matching necklace so you have a set.

Materials

- Silicone crown mold (you can find this on Etsy.com)
- Plasticine or modeling clay
- Two-component clear epoxy resin (look for an ecological, transparent resin that is nontoxic and can be used safely at home)
- Red flowers (dried, preserved, fresh, fabric or paper)
- Small scraps of gold wire (optional)
- Small twigs or leaves (optional)
- Silicone jewelry molds in the shape of quartz, pendants or crystals (you can find these on Etsy.com)
- Thin metal headband
- Fine jewelry wire
- Clear nail polish (optional)
- Jewelry settings for attaching necklace resin pieces (choose a piece that has a small hole or washer and a bell shape that will fit your resin pendants)
- Araldite bicomponent glue
- 10" (25-cm) necklace chain
- Clasp for necklace

Tools

- 2 disposable plastic cups
- Resin mixing sticks
- Fine sandpaper
- Brush for applying resin
- Jeweler's pliers for twisting and cutting wire
- Stick for applying bicomponent glue

1. Because using the whole crown creates a crown with a small circumference, in this project you will only fill half of the mold with resin to make a tiara. To keep the resin from filling the whole mold, fill two of the wells, on opposite sides from each other, with plasticine or modeling clay.

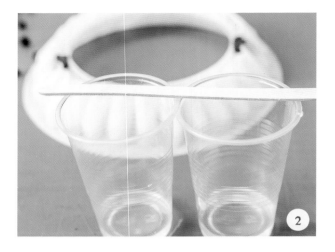

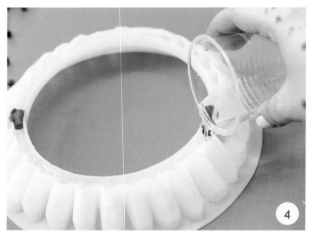

2. Prepare the resin to fill only half of the crown mold. Carefully check the mixing proportions of the components of the resin you are using. Weigh or measure the volumes of each reagent of the resin separately in two disposable plastic cups.

3. Mix the resin with a mixing stick, being careful not to create bubbles.

4. Pour the component mixture slowly into the wells in the crown mold, so that it does not bubble as it falls. Fill the wells only halfway.

5. Place the flowers in the resin. You can add as many as you like. You may also want to add small pieces of gold wire, twigs, leaves or other decorative elements.

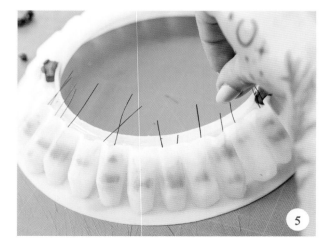

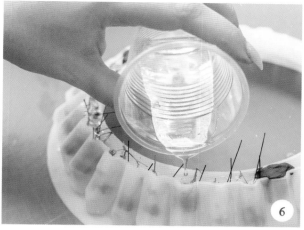

6. After adding the flowers and any other decorations, prepare another pour of resin, following steps 2–3. Pour the resin into the wells of the mold, covering the flowers. You may have to gently push down on the flowers or other decorations so they don't float out of the mold. Allow the resin to cure and solidify for 24 hours.

7. To make the crystals for the necklace, follow steps 2–4, using the silicone jewelry molds.

8. Place matching flowers, gold wire or other pieces inside the molds to match the decorations used in the crown.

9. Follow step 6 to complete the crystals for the necklace.

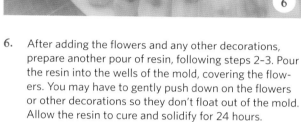

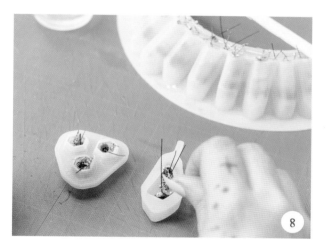

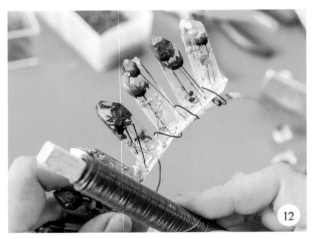

10. Unmold and sand the bottom of the crown to remove any sharp edges or imperfections, until the resin is slightly opaque.

11. Center the resin piece on top of the headband. Wrap the thin jewelry wire first around only the headband, near one end of the resin piece. This will secure the wire to the headband.

12. Then, spiral the thin jewelry wire around the resin crown, attaching the crown to the headband.

13. When you reach the other end, turn the crown over and loop the wire around the crown and headband again until you reach the end where you started; wrapping in both directions will make sure the crown is securely fastened to the headband. Wrap the wire around just the headband several times, then cut the wire using the pliers.

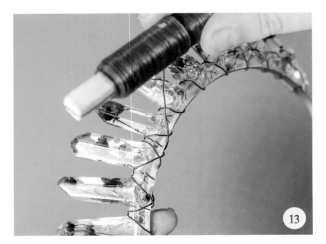

14. Sand the necklace pieces to remove any rough edges. To make the edges clearer after sanding, you can apply more resin mixture with a brush or coat them with transparent nail polish.

15. Select your jewelry findings to set the resin pieces.

16. Pass the thin jewelry wire through the crimp of the finding and create a loop. Cut the wire.

17. Glue the crimp of the finding to the resin pieces with Araldite bicomponent glue. Apply carefully and with a wooden stick, making sure that the glue does not protrude too much and that it is not visible.

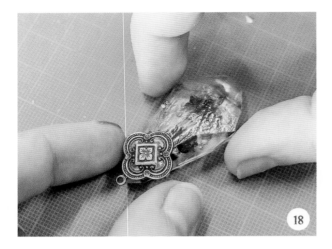

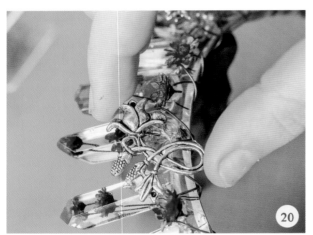

18. Alternatively, add decorations that already have a loop included to join the resin to the necklace.

19. Let the glue dry completely. You can secure the resin pieces in a block of non-staining plasticine or modeling clay while they dry.

20. You can also decorate the outside of the crown with more flowers or metal pieces to match the necklace. Use the same Araldite bicomponent glue to add decorations to the tiara.

21. Cut two 4-inch (10-cm) pieces of the necklace chain and one 2-inch (5-cm) piece.

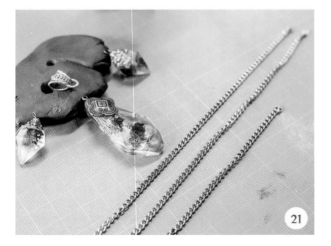

22. On each end of the 2-inch (5-cm) pieces, attach one of the small quartz-shaped resin pieces and one end of one of the 4-inch (10-cm) chains.

23. On the large quartz piece, add a larger crimp or loop so that this main resin piece slides freely on the chain.

24. Attach the necklace clasps of your choice to each end of the chain.

Put It All Together

Hair, Makeup and Other Accessories

Wear as much jewelry as you can to match your dress or outfit to add colorful details to complement the fabric you have chosen.

Wearing bracelets and rings will give you a more regal look. You can also make a metallic belt to match your crown or jewelry.

Carry a sword to knight all the warriors you meet, as if you have just stepped out of the Edmund Leighton painting *The Accolade.*

You can braid your hair or leave it loose with beautiful waves to look like you belong in a pre-Raphaelite painting.

Keep your makeup natural-looking for a more historical, medieval or pre-Raphaelite look.

The Druid

Get Inspired: Celts, Vikings and Fairy Tales

The origin of the druids is mostly priestly or prophetic and dates to the Iron Age or perhaps even earlier. Druids are also mentioned in several medieval tales in which they are portrayed as wise sorcerers. Their name was translated as "knower of the oak" or "seer of the oak" and although there is not much historical data on the subject, they are part of several legends.

Druid instruction was a secret ritual process that took place deep in the forests. Surrounded by mysticism and secrecy, druids are often portrayed as male, but if we believe the myth of Ceridwen, female druids also existed.

Romanticism, neo-paganism and fantasy also add inspiration to the idea of our druid. Druids are popular in heroic fantasy novels or in role-playing games such as Dungeons & Dragons©, which emphasize the concept of druids as magical beings capable of transforming into and communicating with animals, manipulating elements and nature around them and even obtaining healing power from the natural world. This reinterpretation of the mystical sorcerer of the forests is what we have used as a source of inspiration for our druid.

Antlers Headpiece

In this project, you will learn to make your own fantasy headband with two pieces of miniature deer horns modeled, painted and decorated with elements of the forest.

The size of the antlers will determine the weight and comfort of the piece, so for the tutorial example, we have chosen 6-inch (15-cm) horns to create a comfortable headband to wear for a whole day at the fair. When painting your antlers, you can choose to make them as close to nature as possible, or decorate them with fantasy colors, metallic finishes, glitters—the only limit is your imagination! In our example, we chose a fantasy finish metallic green.

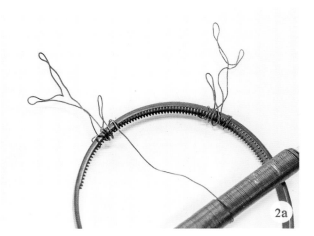

Materials
- Thin jewelry wire
- Plastic headband
- Painter's tape
- Air-dry clay (we used Foam Clay)
- Acrylic paints of your choice
- Moss, flowers and other decorative elements (optional)
- Universal glue

Tools
- Awl, hole punch or modeling tools
- Small paint brushes

1. Search online for deer antlers and draw them on a piece of paper as an outline, sketching the approximate shape and size you would like them to be. Remember that making them too tall or too large will make them heavier or difficult to wear comfortably.

2. Bend pieces of thin jewelry wire in the shape of the antlers you sketched in step 1, then wrap the wire frames around a headband. Make the frames smaller than the size of the antlers you would like, to account for the clay that will be added. Make the shapes as organic as you can, and the two antlers do not have to match exactly.

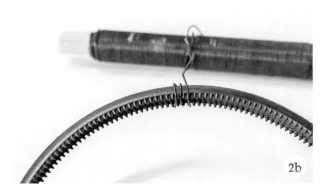

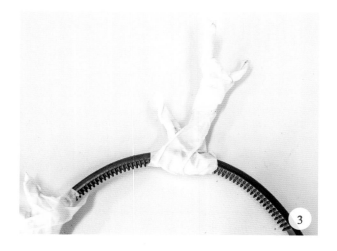

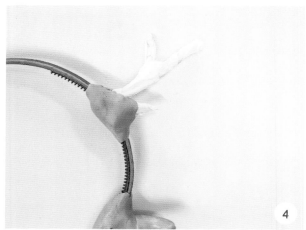

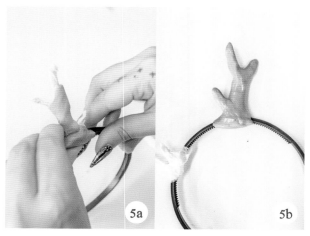

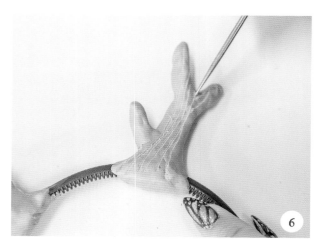

3. Make sure the frames are securely fastened to the headband, then cover the wire antlers and the wrapped part of the headband with painter's tape.

4. Add air-drying clay to the wire antlers and around the wrapped part of the headband. When adding the clay to the headband, make sure to model it with a curve similar to that of the headband so the headband will fit comfortably. Let the clay dry for the recommended time on the clay package instructions so it hardens or polymerizes completely.

5. When the clay is completely dry, add another thin layer of air-drying clay, covering the entire antler frame, including the part that attaches to the headband.

6. Before the new layer of clay dries or polymerizes, use an awl, hole punch or modeling tool to create veins or lines in the antlers to give them a realistic texture. Then, let the clay dry completely.

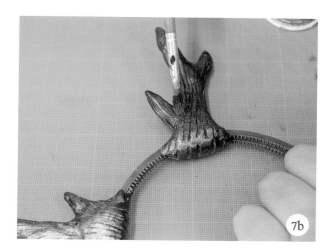

7. Paint the antlers with a layer of acrylic paint. You can use more than one layer of paint if you'd like.

8. Leave the space between the horns plain and covered with your hair or decorate the headpiece with other elements of the forest. You can glue on imitation moss, pine cones, ivy leaves or miniature mushrooms that you purchase or create from air-drying clay.

   The resulting piece fits not only in a druid outfit but can be decorated with other elements or paint finishes to give it a more fanciful touch to complement the look of a winter fairy. Or, sculpt or shape the antlers to look more like those of a goat to transform yourself into a faun!

✵ Hooded Long Cloak ✵

In this project you will learn how to make a cloak a bit different from the hunter's Hooded Wool Capelet (page 47) but also with a hood, because we strongly believe that any garment with it turns out better. The long cloak adds a mystical touch to the druid, especially if you use a color palette that evokes natural settings of the forest or mountains. For this project we have chosen a kind of dark druid, keeping the priestly proto-Celtic inspiration, but in a fantasy context, in which these priests could preach in and about nature.

The length of your cloak will depend on the width of the fabric you choose, as it must be equally long at the front and back with the minimum number of seams to make it easier to assemble. The amount of fabric needed will be double the width of the chosen fabric. For example, if the fabric you choose for this project is 55 inches (140 cm) you will need double that amount in length (110 inches [280 cm]) plus an extra 2 inches (5 cm) of margin.

Materials
* Wool or any other thick fabric in a natural color (see Introduction for amount needed)
* Coat or braid-type fastener or brooches, eyelets, or closure of your choice
* Flat rivets (optional)

Tools
* Measuring tape
* Chalk to mark fabric
* Needle and pins and/or sewing machine
* Eyelet hole punch
* Hand or table riveter

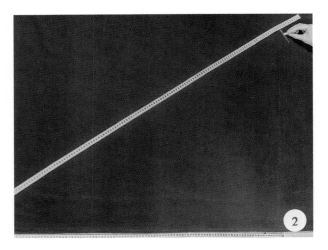

1. Fold your fabric in half along its longest side to make a square.

2. From one of the corners where the fabric is folded on itself, place a measuring tape and mark with a pin or chalk a length of 55 inches (140 cm) or the width of the fabric you chose.

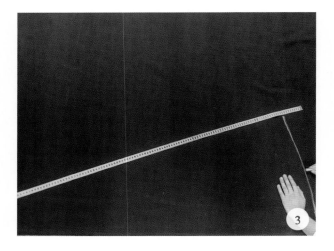

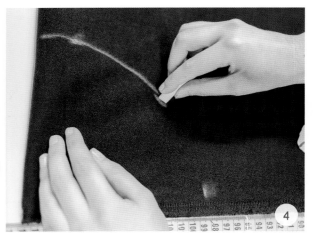

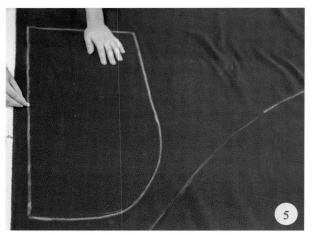

3. Move the measuring tape as if it were the hand of a clock and continue marking the same measurement of the width of the fabric. This will trace a curve from one corner of the fabric to the opposite corner.

4. To trace the neckline, starting at the same corner from which you started on the folded side of the fabric, mark 6 inches (15 cm) at several points and join them together, making a curve drawn with chalk.

5. To draw the pattern for the hood, turn to the project patterns on pages iii–viii. Trace it onto paper and cut it out. Then place the pattern in the triangle of fabric that is left over after drawing the curve in step 3. Cut out the two hood pieces.

6. Join the two pieces of the hood with a French seam (see Techniques & Tricks on page 9). Join the hood to the neck also using a French seam.

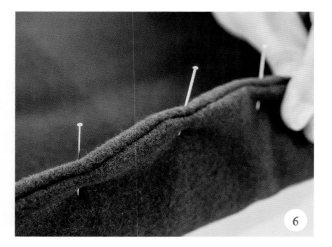

7. Make a ⅜-inch (1-cm) double hem down both sides of the front of the cloak by making two consecutive ⅜-inch (1-cm) folds, then stitching a topstitch seam.

8. Using an overlock or narrow zigzag seam, sew the bottom hem so that the fabric does not fray.

9. Attach your chosen closure to the upper part of the cape. For our project we chose a pair of metal clasps with leather or leatherette pieces that are attached by rivets to the cape. To attach this type of closure, first make holes both in the leather and in the cape, then join them with flat metal rivets.

    You now have your cape to go in pursuit of ancestral inspiration! As we have seen in the other tutorials in this book, changing the color, the fabric (thickness, sheen) or the type of fastener (eyelets, fasteners or snaps) will result in a quite different garment you can create to match other outfits.

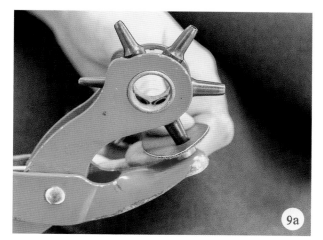

Log Bag

In this project we will create a leather bag with the shape and texture of a log, as if we had found a piece of wood resting among the pine needles in the middle of the forest. This bag is the ideal complement for the druid's costume, whether to store fruits, seeds, herbs or some other possessions during a Ren faire. As this is a piece inspired by an element present in nature, make sure the finishes or cuts are not forced or artificial. There's no need to achieve a perfect or homogeneous finish; instead, try for irregularities so the piece has a more organic appearance.

The size of the bag is up to you. We have given suggestions for size in the Materials list. However, if you want a larger or smaller bag, the rest of the materials should change as well. To change the size, measure the circumference of the wooden circle pieces you will be using as the sides of the bag. The total length of the leather sheet must be 4 inches (10 cm) longer than the circumference of the sides, so that the top flap of the bag overlaps the bottom. The width of the bag can be whatever you would like. The example shown in the photographs has a width of 8¼ inches (21 cm).

Materials
- 1 (8¼ x 10" [21 x 25-cm]) leather sheet, ⅛" (3 mm) thick
- Leather dye (we used Pro Dye in brown and green)
- 1 yard (1 m) leather strip, 1–2" (2.5–5 cm) wide
- Contact glue
- 2 (6" [15-cm]) wooden circles (such as wooden coasters, or ask in a home improvement store for a custom cut of wood)
- 12 (⅜" [1-cm]) nails or screws
- 1 buckle horn lock clasp (or closure of your choice)
- 4 pairs of brass rivets

Tools
- Black marker or pencil
- Leather cutter or scalpel
- Awl or beveler
- Sponge or a piece of cotton or wool fabric for applying the dye
- Brush for applying the glue
- Hammer or screwdriver
- Eyelet hole punch
- Hand or table riveter

1

1. Using a marker, create a rough-looking edge down the outside edges of the leather, making the edge curving and undulating, reminiscent of the texture of the bark of a tree. Use a leather cutter or scalpel to follow the rough edge you marked, making superficial cuts or incisions on the outside edges of the leather. Make sure that the cuts are no more than ⅜ inch (1 cm) long, but don't be afraid to make as many as you want. You can also use a tool like an awl or beveler to trim the edges or deepen the marks in some areas.

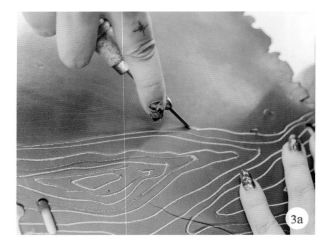

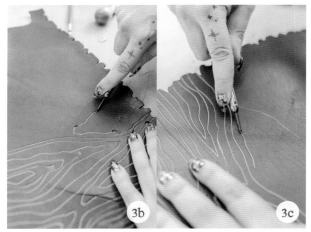

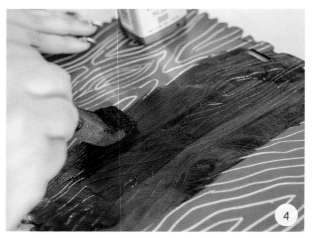

2. Using a leather cutter or scalpel, make two slits in the leather strip for the strap for the bag. They will be at the top of the bag when it is assembled, to accommodate the straps. Make the slits a little longer and wider than the strap you have chosen, and they should be located about 1 inch (2.5 cm) in from each outer edge and at one-third of the length of the leather piece.

3. To simulate a wooden texture in the rest of the piece, connect the notches you made on the edges from one side to the other using the leather cutter. Use thin lines and do not cut through the leather. Make the lines organic, curved and fluid and create some knots with irregular and concentric circles, such as those in real wood.

4. Apply the dye with a rag or sponge. We first applied a layer of medium brown, to unify the tone. Apply the same dye to the leather strap.

5. Let the first layer of dye dry completely. Then, apply a second layer (we used a dark brown tone) along the edges of the leather sheet and through the lines, to give more visual depth to the piece. Let the leather dry completely.

6. Apply contact glue to the edges of the wooden circles. Very carefully attach the leather sheet along the glued contour of the circular pieces, leaving ¼ inch (6 mm) of the irregular edges of the leather sticking out on the outsides of the wooden pieces. Stop gluing when there are about 3½ inches (9 cm) of the circular pieces unglued. The remaining unglued leather will form the flap of the bag. Let the glue dry completely.

7. To secure the leather to the wooden pieces, nail (or screw in) a few small nails (or screws) around the circumference of the circles. Nail (or screw) as straight as possible so that the nails or screws do not stick out the sides.

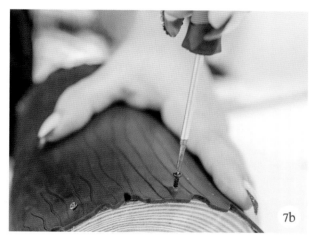

8. Insert one end of the leather into one of the slits you made in step 2. Nail (or screw) the leather strap to the inside face of one of the wooden pieces. Repeat this step with the other end of the leather strap and the other wooden piece.

9. Using a marker or pencil, mark where you would like to place the buckle horn lock clasp on the flap and the body of the bag. Attach both sides of the clasp using the brass rivets.

Now your bag is ready to go for exploring the forest, and collecting acorns, pine cones or mushrooms. But remember not to leave it on the ground or you might lose it because you mistook it for a real log!

∼ Animal-Shaped Mask ∼

The druids used their talents in the service of knowledge in a wide variety of fields. Posidonius revealed that they were mainly devoted to "physiology" (i.e., natural sciences, such as physics, chemistry, geology, botany and zoology). According to Pliny the Elder, the druids classified plant and animal species and studied in which form they could use them.

Therefore, we have added an animal mask to our druid. We chose the fox, which is one of the most revered and appreciated animal totems. They are not only beautiful, but they have been considered spiritual animals for creative people or those who are going through complicated situations, since one of the teachings of the fox in folk tales and legends is that it is able to gracefully get out of any kind of predicament with wit and trickery.

Materials
- 1 (8" [20-cm]) leather sheet, ⅛" (3 mm) thick
- Acrylic leather paint (we used Angelus in white and black or dark brown)
- 2 (12" [30-cm]) lengths of ribbon, cord or string

Tools
- Scissors
- Leather cutter or scalpel
- 2 paint brushes (one medium-small, one small)
- Sponge for applying and blending paint
- Leather hole punch

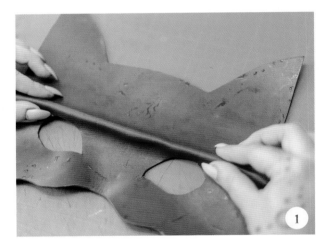

1. Turn to the project pattern on page vi for this piece. Trace it onto paper and cut it out. Draw the pattern onto the leather piece with a leather cutter or scalpel. Cut out the shape and eye holes. Moisten the leather (but don't get it fully wet) and while damp, shape it by pinching it with your fingers over the cuts of the eyes to make a frown, with a prominent fold outward.

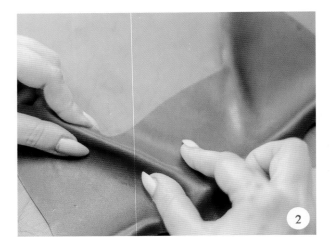

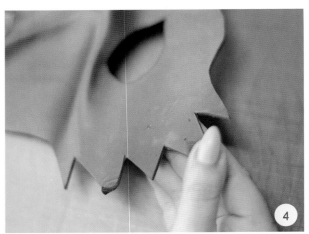

2. Pinch folds upward from the center of the eyes diagonally toward the ears.

3. While the piece is still damp, add another pinch at the level of the nose to give the nose volume.

4. Turn or twist some of the corners or peaks of the mask to give it more realism and three-dimensionality.

5. With white acrylic paint (or similar paint for leather or fabric) and a medium–small paint brush, paint the cheeks or whiskers of the fox.

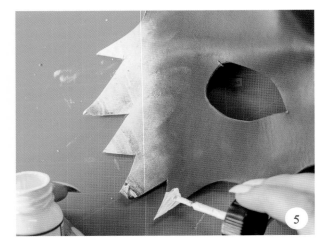

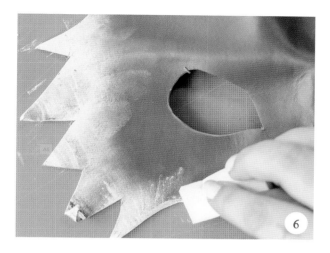

6. Using a small sponge, diffuse the white paint upward and downward toward the inside of the mask.

7. With the same paint and a smaller brush, paint a small triangle on the tip of each ear at the outermost end, blending inward as well.

8. Also paint white on the sides and lower part of the beard or whiskers that have been twisted inward.

9. With black or dark brown paint also suitable for leather, paint the inside of the eye. You can add a corner of the eye on the sides to give it more expressiveness.

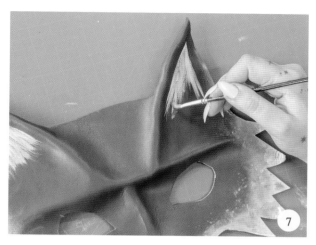

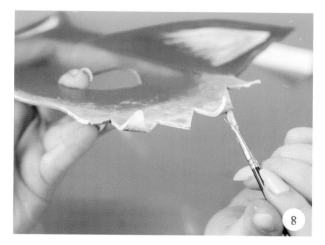

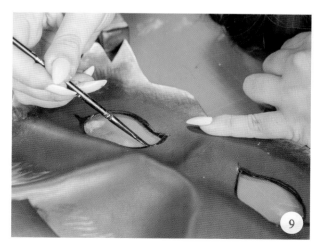

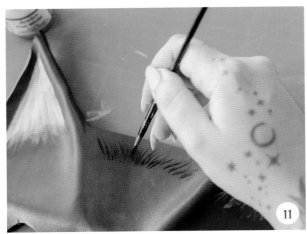

10. Trace the whiskers of the fox with dark paint, using the small brush.

11. Between the ears, in the center, draw some short hairs.

12. On each side of the mask, a little above the height of your ears, use a hole punch to create holes. Tie a ribbon or string to each hole to use to adjust the mask to fit your head.

These same processes and techniques can be applied to create masks of other types of animals. You can find lots of simple animal mask patterns on Etsy.com. You can use black leather to create a raven mask, white leather to make yourself an owl and so on.

Horned Raven Skull Necklace

Through this project you will learn how to make your own druid, wizard or witch necklaces, using real pieces easily found in the forest, or small pieces you can buy or create.

For our druid character we have created a necklace that looks like the remains of an animal collected and processed as if it were a magical talisman. In the example images, we have started from a resin copy of a raven skull, but you could use the head that best suits your character.

Materials
- Thin jewelry wire
- Painter's tape
- Air-dry clay (we used Foam Clay)
- Acrylic paints of your choice
- Plastic or real small bird skull (you can find these in a toy shop or on Etsy.com)
- Universal glue
- Moss, leaves and other decorative elements
- Bitumen of Judea or Syrian asphalt
- Small eyebolt
- ½ yard (½ m) leather or suede strip

Tools
- Awl, hole punch or modeling tools
- Small brushes in several different sizes
- Dremel tool

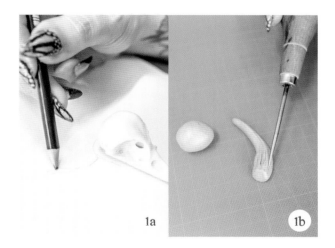

1a   1b

2

1. Using thin jewelry wire, create some small horns, following steps 2-6 of the Antlers Headpiece project on pages 91-92 (although the horns for this project should be smaller so they match the size of the skull you choose, without standing out too much).

2. Glue the horns on either side of the small skull and then add air-drying clay over the horns. Using an awl, add texture so the horns appear to come out of the skull. Another option is to disguise the joints between the horns and the skull by gluing on pieces of moss or small leaves, etc.

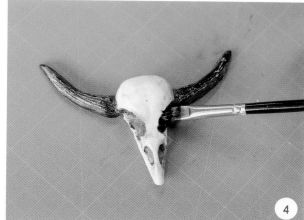

3. Paint the whole piece in cream or bone color.

4. With brown acrylic paint or Bitumen of Judea add shadows at the base of the horns and in the cavities of the skull. Allow the paint to dry completely.

5. Make a small hole with the Dremel tool in the center of the skull, then screw in a small eyebolt with a ring to hang it.

6. Thread the leather or suede strap through the eyelet and close the necklace with a sliding knot.

   And that's it! Your druid talisman is ready. Remember that you can decorate it or add other pieces hanging at different heights on the string or necklace to make it more ornate.

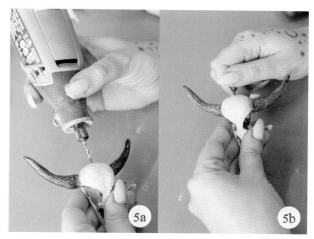

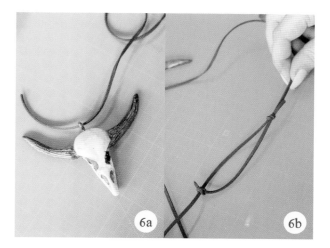

Put It All Together

Hair, Makeup and Other Accessories

You could also try creating a different version of a druid using white tones for the clothes and makeup or creating a mask with a more traditional look.

Under your mask, you can apply markings with Celtic or Viking symbolism using makeup.

To be a druid like the powerful wizards of the Welsh forests, we recommend making your own staff using elements that you can find in nature such as branches, horns, pebbles or ropes.

Don't forget to add natural elements to your outfit such as fur, horns or acorns that will help show that your druid is in tune with nature.

If you have long hair, make several braids of different thicknesses, or make French or Dutch braids and decorate them with metal or wooden beads at the end or between the braids.

Creating Your Own Character

Use colored eyeliner to add lines, dots or other drawings on your skin to add a more mystical or fantasy look to your character.

The peasant's Chemise Underdress (page 33) can be made in a lot of colors; for example, use green combined with a tartan-checked bodice to create a Scottish *Outlander*-style outfit.

You can also make the peasant's Chemise Underdress (page 33) with baroque brocade fabrics for a royalcore or regency-inspired style as seen in the television show *Bridgerton*.

For a Ren-faire style Little Red Riding Hood look: Use red wool to make a short capelet like the hunter's Hooded Wool Capelet (page 47), then have someone else wear the Animal-Shaped Mask (page 102).

The princess's Velvet Royal Dress (page 73), with the right accessories and different colors, can make you look as though you are coming out of an elven village or Middle Earth.

Change the print of the fairy's Maxiskirt (page 17) using other textures or different patterns to create other types of fantasy beings or even sorceresses or dryads.

The pattern of the druid's Hooded Long Cloak (page 94) can be used to make a style closer to royalcore, to a princess, a prince or a noble ready to attend a regency ball, using shiny fabrics, such as satin or crepe.

The hunter's Medieval Linen Shirt (page 51) in other colors, fabrics or lengths is ideal for a royalcore prince, a fairy court prince or even a pirate.

Acknowledgments

About the Authors

Thanks to Victor Plata, for helping us so much with the photography of the tutorials and for being such a wonderful model. To Mel, for lending us her hands in some of the textile processes. To Ylenia and Gemma, for posing for us as some of the characters. To Ma Ángeles and Jordi of Raser Disseny, for helping us digitize our textile patterns and to Jafet from Outcast Props, for helping us digitize our leather patterns.

As for the book creation process, thanks to the author Concepción Perea for advising us in our first publishing adventure, to Carlos of Carcreatures for helping us with some English revisions when we already had our Spanish brains melted and to Bea from 13th Psyche for giving us a hand with the graphic design.

And a giant and massive THANK-YOU to all our customers and followers around the world who have allowed us, with their constant support, to develop our creativity and continue growing together.

Alassie is the heart and soul of the Costurero Real brand and its CEO and director. She was born in the south of Spain, in Granada. Both her grandmothers were seamstresses and they taught her how to pattern, design and sew when she was 15 years old. She started studying law at university, but due to a genetic illness, she was forced to abandon her studies. When her situation stabilized, she started to search for other things to study that would make her happy and found a high education in textile and fashion design, between 2005 and 2008, first at the School of Arts in Granada, studying textile arts and fashion design, and then at the IED (European Institute of Design) where she studied costume design for cinema and theatre. In 2008 she came to Barcelona to continue studying and began accepting custom orders she sewed at home. In 2012 she rented a small workshop in Hospitalet de Llobregat (Barcelona) and the project began to grow.

Mara von Entropy is a biologist born in the north of Spain, from the province where the best red wine is produced (in her words) and a region where the darkest fairy tales are still in popular memory. She joined Alassie's project almost a decade ago, to bring order to the team. She started managing shipments, helping with emails, assisting Alassie with sewing and other projects, and nowadays is often buried under mountains of numbers and Excel spreadsheets. Her university background is purely scientific, but her knowledge of botany and mycology along with her adoration of fantasy, folklore and mythology made her a perfect fit for the Royal Seamstress project. She is a book lover, so when she is not working, she is organizing themed events in Barcelona or reading a fantasy book with a glass of wine nearby and a couple of cats.

Index

Page numbers in **boldface** indicate illustrations.